Horse

Chinese

Horoscope

2023

By
IChingHun FengShuisu

Table of Contents

Introduce

The character of people born in the year of the HORSE

People born this year like to talk, talk wisely, and have a lot of patience. You can endure any problem, no matter how difficult it is, without complaining in front of others. You enjoy making the best use of your physical strength. When you want something, you usually do it yourself unless you have lofty goals. Hardworking, not passive, always alert, enjoys being the center of attention, enjoys attending social events, participate in almost all sports, enjoys traveling, and enjoys competition. You are self-centered, despise conventions, and are cunning rather than clever. People born in this year value freedom, dislike being forced to do things they don't want to do and are willing to give up everything for love.

Strength:
You get along well with others and are respected by them, brave.

Weaknesses:

You have a bad temper and frequently cause harm to others for no reason.

Love:
This year's babies are very attractive. Their love is not showy, but it is constant. It could be said that there are people who come almost every day to flirt and say nice things, and who would like others to come and take care of them. People born in this year dislike inconsistent people. A good-looking person with a narcissistic personality, on the other hand, is constantly thinking about how handsome or beautiful you are. People born in this year believe that they must be the only ones, so if you enjoy being pampered, you can be confident that you can permanently bind your lover.

Suitable Career:
People born in the Year of the Horse are fire-elemental, so they should pursue a career that matches their destiny, and their ability to promote progress, prosperity, and profit. Education, research, occupation, teacher,

doctor, administrator, beautician, gas station, photographer, shop selling stationery, all types of electrical equipment or handicrafts, selling artificial flowers, selling cloth, selling drugs, and creating publishing houses are all careers that will suit your luck. It was fated for you to be born in the Year of the Horse.

Year of the HORSE (Water) | (1942) & (2002)

"The Horse that travels " is a person born in the year of the HORSE at the age of 81 years (1942) and 22 years (2002)

Overview

For this generation's young destiny If you go to do any activities or travel this year, it is because the planet that enters the house of destiny this year is "star across the sky." Accidents, especially those involving heat and fire, should be avoided at all costs. Metal tools, equipment, sharp objects, and other sharp objects can cause injury, bleeding, and rubber out. You should find an opportunity to pay respects to the gods and pay respects to the god Tai asks to protect him from all dangers at the start of the year.

Career and Business

Even if the elders violate the feng shui principles, they will be blessed by the auspicious stars. As a result, work and business activities are expected to run smoothly. You have nothing to be concerned about. There will also be assistance in carrying out the various projects. If you intend to study this year, apply to the youth destiny. Other activities do not require much time. It will result in remarkable progress. Especially this month, which has been outstanding in both work and education. For both the destiny, the age is 1st month of China (4 Feb. – 5 Mar.), the 6th month of China (7 Jul. – 7 Aug.), the 8th month of China (8 Sep. – 7 Oct.), and the 9th month of China (8 Oct – 6 Nov.), but if entering the following months, including the 12th month of China (5 Jan. – 3 Feb.), the 2nd month of China (6 Mar. – 4 Apr.), the 5th month China (6 Jun. – 6 Jul.), and 11th month of China (7 Dec. 22 – 5 Jan. 23). There will be disagreements over personnel management. Elders must be impartial. Assign the job based on the skills of the person doing it. The work will be done correctly and will not cause any harm. Furthermore, the contract documents must thoroughly examine the finer details. Be cautious of hidden objects as they can cause harm.

Financial

The senior's financial fortunes have been quite volatile this year. If you're still working, you'll have to work a little harder to make this year's money. But when the money comes in, there's always a reason to spend it. Furthermore, there will be numerous leak points and a lack of liquidity in the circulation system for many months. Especially during the following months: the 12th month of China (5 Jan. – 3 Feb.), the 2nd month of China (6 Mar. – 4 Apr.), the 5th month of China (6 Jun. – 6 Jul.), and the 11th month of China (7 Dec. 22 – 5 Jan. 23) that the fate should avoid lending money to others or issuing financial guarantees, as well as gambling, gambling, and speculating on various aspects. Do not be greedy and greedy for other people's property. Instead, take care not to lose your own. Do not engage in illegal or immoral business to keep your liquidity. They are the months in which the fortune and money of destiny have good liquidity: 1st month of China (4 Feb. – 5 Mar.), 6th month of China (7 Jul. – 7 Aug.), 8th month of China (8 Sep. – 7 Oct.) and 9th month of China (8 Oct. – 6 Nov.)

Family

You have received auspicious power to visit your home this year, so there is a requirement to organize auspicious events for your children. Moving to a new place of employment is auspicious. Auspicious decorations, renovations, and people's success stories in the house. However, due to the negative influence of "Pang Hou" (White Tiger), which has been in focus, unexpected disasters and accidents will occur. Accidents must be avoided both at home and while traveling. Both have criteria for having problems with lawsuits or government agencies. Especially during the following months that need to increase caution in unforeseen events, namely, the 12th month of China (5 Jan. – 3 Feb.), the 2nd month of China (6 Mar. – 4 Apr.), the 5th month of China (6 Jun

– 6 Jul), and 11th month of China (7 Dec. 22 – 5 Jan. 23). Be wary of troublemakers who are minors or domestic servants. Also, be aware that fainting or stumbling may result in injury. They should be cautious of misplaced valuables.

Love

Senior Master's romantic life is heading in the right direction, with compassion and understanding. This year is thus appropriate for taking spouses on a trip to distant lands to help strengthen relationships or going to temples to continue making merit, assisting in enhancing luck in many things to proceed in a better direction.

If you have recently shown a lack of concern for your lover's spouse. This year, if you have something to say or express, it's a good time to show sincerity to compensate for a lack of love. As for the month in which the love of the young destiny will be born, the monsoon is the 12th month of China (5 Jan. – 3 Feb.), the 2nd month of China (6 Mar. – 4 Apr.), the 5th month of China (6 Jun. – 6 Jul) and the 11th month of China (7 Dec 22 – 5 Jan 23).

Health

The Elder Fate's health was deteriorating as a result of the numerous evil stars perched on the Destroyer Clan. As a result, this year, you must prioritize your health and avoid accidents. Be wary of the hidden diseases that will emerge this year. As a result, if you suspect that something is wrong with your body, you should see a doctor right away to get a diagnosis so that treatment can begin as soon as possible. You didn't want Elder to be too concerned, though. Because there is an auspicious star "Ngwe Tek" to support and assist in the house of fate. The disease has a high chance of being cured. For the young destiny, be wary of mishaps on the road and of the dangers of heat and fire. Be wary of joining a bad group of friends who will cause you problems. This includes being cautious of metal equipment and sharp objects. Especially during the month in which the destiny, both age cycles must add special attention, including the 12th month of China (5 Jan. – 3 Feb.), the 2nd month of China (6 Mar. – 4 Apr.), 5th month of China (6 Jun. – 6

Jul.) and 11th month of China (7 Dec. 22 – 5 Jan. 23).

Year of the HORSE (Wood) | (1954) & (2014)

" The HORSE in the grass " is a person born in the year of the HORSE at the age of 69 years (1954) and 9 years (2014)

Overview

Because the planet that orbits into the Year of the Horse's destiny this year is the "star across the sky," this year will have both good and bad mixed in with half of the work. It is not easy for those of you who are in business to make a lot of money. As a result, to keep your business running smoothly, you should constantly build and strengthen relationships with your contacts. You should always be expanding your knowledge to adapt to the current situation and avoid becoming lost in the crowd. Another thing that should be your number one priority this year is your health. Be wary of hidden dangers, particularly diseases affecting the liver, kidneys, intestines, and stomach. You should choose to eat more this year. Avoid foods that have been grilled, grilled, or barbecued. To stay healthy, you should exercise regularly, get enough rest, and eat nutritious foods. Traveling long distances should be done with caution, as injuries to the hands, arms, and legs can occur, and the use of road vehicles should not be taken lightly. As a result, in this round at the start of the year, you should find an opportunity to pay respect to the gods, ask for blessings, and pay tribute to the gods of Tai. You should make time throughout the year to make merit and make merit to help fill in the gaps and alleviate disasters.

For the destiny of the young Star, the warlord is the planet orbiting this year's destiny house. This year, be cautious of accidents that may result in injuries. Parents should take their children to pay homage to the gods at the start of the year. Pay your respects to Lord Tai for him to protect you. and avoid dangers that may arise unexpectedly.

Career and Business

This year, even in the field of work, including business, there will be bumps in the road. However, having a good relationship with those around you and constantly improving yourself to keep up with the current situation will help you overcome the various obstacles. If the work is well planned ahead of time, the resource factors are readily available, and even the most difficult situations can be overcome. But should be more interested in 12 months of China (5 Jan. – 3 Feb.), the 2nd month of China (6 Mar. – 4 Apr.), the 5th month of China (6 Jun. – 6 Jul), and the 11th month of China (7 Dec. 22 – 5 Jan. 23), which is the month that trade will face problems. Destiny must be more cautious when dealing with outside work that will present obstacles and internal conflicts. Also, be cautious when signing contracts related to work or business; there is a risk of damage. The month in which the direction of work and investment this year is prosperous and bright are 1st months of China (4 Feb. - 5 Mar.), the 6th months of China (7 Jul. - 7 Aug.), The 8th month of China (8 Sep. – 7 Oct.) and the 9th months of China (8 Oct. – 6 Nov.).

Financial

The fortunes of the Year of the Horse have been influenced by evil stars this year, resulting in some liquidity shortages. Although regular cash flows from salaries or sales of goods or services will continue to flow in at normal levels. However, unexpected events frequently interfere with the destiny to lose money in trivial matters. as well as the tale of the floating fortune from gambling It would be difficult to anticipate because it would be futile. For the month when the financial star is down And you should manage your income and expenses prudently, namely: 12th month of China (5 Jan. - 3 Feb.), 2nd month of China (6 Mar. - 4 Apr.), 5th month of China (6 Jun. – 6 Jul.) and 11th month of China (7 Dec. 22 – 5 Jan. 23) should abstain from gambling and gamble Don't lend money while expecting investment guarantees. This year, you should think about readiness in all aspects, as well as money rotation throughout the investment period. You should also select a month that is favorable to your fortune. The month that your financial fortune has good liquidity, such as the 1st month of China (4 Feb. – 5 Mar.), the 6th month of China (7 Jul. – 7 Aug.), the 8th month of China. (8 Sep. – 7 Oct.), and the 9th month of China (8 Oct. – 6 Nov.).

Family

The family horoscope, despite the auspicious power that will visit your home this year, will be hampered by an unfortunate power. As a result, the auspicious path is not always easy. It's beneficial to mix with undesirables. Especially during the months that you need to be careful and pay special attention to your family, such as the 12th month of China (5 Jan. - 3 Feb.), the 2nd month of China (6 Mar. - 4 Apr), the 5th month of China (6 Jun - 6 Jul) and the 11th month of China (7 Dec 22 - 5 Jan 23), which if your family has planned many auspicious events. It can help to lessen the power of unlucky stars. Furthermore, during such times, one should be aware of unforeseen events. Accidents, and health issues for the elderly and children at home. Furthermore, they should be cautious of their relatives or minors causing trouble and arguing with neighbors until the problem spreads.

Love

This year, love is good at the beginning and end of the year, but there are often misunderstandings that cause feuds between the two of you in the middle of the year. Be wary of being enamored with a fleeting love that will lead to a breakup. Going out to parties with friends or entertainment venues, in particular, will cause problems and arguments with the members of the house. The months in which the love of destiny is quite fragile and easy to argue are the 12th month of China (5 Jan. - 3 Feb.), the 2nd month of China (6 Mar. - 4 Apr.), the 5th month of China (6 Jun - 6 Jul) and the 11th month of China (7 Dec 22 - 5 Jan 23). Please refrain from visiting entertainment venues. and should not interfere with the family of others.

Health

This year's fate is not in good health. Be on the lookout for health issues involving the liver, kidneys, and other hidden diseases that may emerge this year. May fate avoid hot and grilled foods such as barbecue and satay, as well as all evil things. Cigarettes and alcohol, in particular, should be consumed in moderation. Especially during the months that you need to be more careful, namely, the 12th month of China (5 Jan. - 3 Feb.), the 2nd month of China (6 Mar. - 4 Apr), the 5th month of China (6 Jun - 6 Jul) and the 11th month of China (7 Dec 22 - 5 Jan 23), where you must avoid driving and driving if you go to a party and drink alcohol. After drinking, you should be cautious with your words because they may offend others, resulting in unanticipated events. As a result, you should be extra cautious this year if you notice anything wrong with your body. You should see a doctor right away.

Year of the HORSE (Fire) | (1966)

" The Horse in stall " is a person born in the year of the HORSE at the age of 57 years (1966)

Overview

For the Year of the Horse, you will be counted as one of the main zodiac signs "Heng" at this age, even this year, because auspicious stars "Thep Satai" and "The Virtue Star" are orbiting to shine in the house of fate. A bright ray of light appeared to save the day. As a result, in terms of financial fortune, there will be good cash inflows, and job duties will progress. The trade business will thrive. However, there are still obstacles in the way of work progress. It is a source of stress and disease that will follow. The importance of health and underlying disease cannot be overstated. Hard work and insufficient rest can cause headaches and insomnia. It also has an effect on work efficiency, which will be reduced. Accidents should be avoided this year, in addition to health concerns. Both at work and on the road. Chao Ta must be wary of arguments and lawsuits in this year's family. Because your birth year is considered one of the zodiac signs, "Heng," if you have time at the beginning of the year, you should pay respect to the gods to ask for blessings and pay respect to the Tai tribute gods. Make merit and make merit. The merit will aid in relaxing and lightening the misfortune.

Career and Business

Because of the power of the auspicious stars shining, the fortunes of this age are bright. Job responsibilities will grow, and trade will thrive. This is an excellent time to expand your portfolio, boost your productivity, expand your market, or increase your external investment. Even if it falls during the wedding ceremony year, this is still a good opportunity. It will be a shame if you let it pass without doing anything. But when stepping into the following months, work will face obstacles and you need to be more careful, for example, during the 12th month of China (5 Jan. - 3 Feb.), the 2nd month of China (6 Mar. – 4 Apr.) 5th month of China (6 Jun. – 6 Jul.) and 11th month of China (7 Dec. 22 – 5 Jan. 23). Be wary of coordination issues. To arrange people to work, you must select the right people for the job; otherwise, you will cause harm. Be wary of conflicts, as well as misrepresentation or misleading employees. And should avoid investing large sums during the 5th month of China (6 Jun. - 6 Jul.) and the 11th month of China (7 Dec. 22 - 5 Jan. 23). Work and investment are smooth and bright, including 1st month of China (4 Feb. – 5 Mar.), 6th month of China (7 Jul. – 7 Aug.), 8th month of China (8 Sep. – 7 Oct.) and the 9th month of China (8 Oct. – 6 Nov.).

Financial

The fortune teller's fortune will be favorable this year. Both cash inflows are direct. You increase your investment in other areas by using your salary, product sales, or income. Investment is heading in the right direction. The rates of return are adequate. However, you should be cautious not to lose money in unexpected circumstances during the month of the financial downturn. which is the 12th month of China (5 Jan. - 3 Feb.), the 2nd month of China (6 Mar. - 4 Apr.) 5th month of China (6 Jun. - 6 Jul.), and the 11th month of China (7 Dec. 22 - 5 Jan. 23). Avoid lending money or accepting guarantees, and stay away from businesses that are suspected of being illegal or high-risk. because there is a risk of bodily harm and property loss.

Family

Overall, the family's luck this year has been good on the outside but bad on the inside. Even though the house has auspicious power, there are evil stars who send power to harass. The primary concern should be the health of family members, particularly the elderly in the household. as well as problems with arguing and unrest in the home. Especially during the months of unrest, such as the 12th month of China (5 Jan. – 3 Feb.), the 2nd month of China (6 Mar. – 4 Apr.), the 5th month of China (6 Jun - 6 Jul), and the 11th month of China (7 Dec 22 - 5 Jan 23), where fate must find a way to prevent. Because there is a presumption that valuables will be misplaced or stolen. Be cautious of disturbing servants both inside and outside. Be aware that there will be a disagreement until it becomes a major lawsuit.

Love

The love horoscope for this year is favorable. You will be able to go on a sightseeing trip with your lover or spouse to make you feel more at ease, allowing you to discuss and improve your understanding of what is owed. As a result, the warm and sweet relationship returns to happiness. However, you should keep the important day in mind and schedule regular family activities. Fill in the gaps in your love and don't let it fall apart because this year will have the power of manners intervene, causing destiny to fall in love with temporary love. Take care that third parties do not influence your family and disrupt the peace of the household. Especially during the month when love is fragile and you need to be careful of arguments, such as the 12th month of China (5 Jan. - 3 Feb.), the 2nd month of China (6 Mar. - 4 Apr.), 5th month of China (6 Jun. – 6 Jul.) and 11th month of China (7 Dec. 22 – 5 Jan 23).

Health

Destiny's overall health was quite good. Although there are some illnesses, they are not concerning. However, to strengthen your immune system, you should always take care of your health. Because if you get sick, your ability to work will suffer. As a result, you should exercise regularly and get plenty of rest. Take care of your food and eat hygienically. If you're having a bad month, you should prioritize your health. Especially during the 12th month of China (5 Jan. – 3 Feb.), the 2nd month of China (6 Mar. – 4 Apr.), the 5th month of China (6 Jun. – 6 Jul.) and the 11th month of China (7 Dec. 22 – 5 Jan. 23) should be careful of gastroenteritis, food poisoning, including traveling. We also ask that you always keep safety in mind. Don't undervalue the best.

Year of the HORSE (Earth) | (1978)

" The horse in the stable " is a person born in the year of the HORSE at the age of 45 years (1978)

Overview

Although people born in the Year of the Horse (Horse) this year will be counted as one of the fall zodiac signs "Heng," they may not be able to block the good trade opportunities that you deserve. You simply need to increase your determination and diligence. However, during the year, evil stars "Tribute Pua" (Star Time) appeared and began to harass the house of destiny. What should be considered is that there may be a job relocation, job relocation, and business obstacles that will affect family peace. People in the house frequently have things that give them headaches or unexpected events that irritate and annoy them. Because this year is designed to be a joint year. You should be able to pay homage to the Lord Tai Tribute at the start of the year. (Annual horoscope guardian deities) or go to the temple to worship the sacred things you revere to receive blessings. Make merit after merit to help mitigate misfortune and promote your work to run smoothly.

Career and Business

The event will not take place this year. Meet the client. You will be assisted and supported for the work to proceed smoothly. What you must remember is to remember the worth of those who offer assistance and to be cautious with your words and actions, not to be aggressive, but to be respectful and humble. It will aid in the completion of many tasks. In particular, the months in which your work and trade will be smooth and prosperous include the 1st month of China (4 Feb. – 5 Mar.), the 6th month of China (7 Jul. – 7 Aug.), the 8th month of China (8 Sep. – 7 Oct.) and the 9th month of China (8 Oct. – 6 Nov.), but if stepping into the 12th month of China (5 Jan. – 3 Feb.), the 2nd month of China (6 Mar. – 4 Apr.), the 5th month of China (6 Jun. – 6 Jul.) and the 11th month of China (7 Dec. 22 – 5 Jan. 23) that the work will become stuck, that there will be obstacles and problems, and that you should exercise caution in both your actions and your words. It will also hurt the spread of other issues.

Financial

For the fortune teller's fortune this year, the first six months will be difficult to spin money, with less liquidity. However, cash inflows will continue to flow in the second half of the year, providing you with more income both directly and through various channels. However, the fortunes of gambling are not always predictable or dedicated. It's simple to come and simple to leave. In particular, in the month when the financial star fell, liquidity was tight, such as the 12th month of China (5 Jan. – 3 Feb.), the 2nd month of China (6 Mar. – 4 Apr), the 5th month of China (6 Jun. – 6 Jul.) and the 11th month of China (7 Dec. 22 – 5 Jan.23) prohibit gambling and gambling. Borrowing and taking guarantees are illegal. Be wary of accounting errors that can lead to a lack of liquidity.

As for the month that your finances will return to have good liquidity, such as the 1st month of China (4 Feb. – 5 Mar.), the 6th month of China (7 Jul. – 7 Aug.), the 8th month of China (8 Sep. – 7 Oct.) and 9th month of China (8 Oct. – 6 Nov.).

Family
This year, auspicious power came to visit the family. There may be auspicious events at home that make moving into a new house auspicious. There will be important visitors to the house. But be careful during the following months in which the family will experience chaos: 12th month of China (5 Jan. – 3 Feb.), 2nd month of China (6 Mar. – 4 Apr.), 5th month

of China (6 Jun. - 6 Jul.) and 11th month of China (7 Dec. 22 - 5 Jan. 23) Be wary of valuables that have been misplaced or stolen. Be wary of minors or subordinates who cause damage, loss of property, or cause arguments. In addition, accidents in the home, particularly with the elderly, should be avoided.

Relatives and friends are reasonable. Even though I am fortunate to have helpful friends. However, some malicious individuals are secretly attacking you. Also, be wary of being exploited and the hope of profiting solely from you. Especially during the following bad months: 12th month of China (5 Jan. – 3 Feb.), 2nd month of China (6 Mar. – 4 Apr.), 5th month of China (6 Jun. – 6 Jul.), and 11th month of China (7 Dec. 22 – 5 Jan. 23).

Love

Your love horoscope is hot this year. Love is not always easy. They may lose consciousness and fall in love with a temporary love that is not true love as a result of being influenced by the power of manners, Huai (Charm). Furthermore, be wary of third-party issues that may interfere with the path of love. There will be miscommunications and disagreements. Especially during the months when you need to increase care and take care of each other to avoid fragile love, such as the 12th month of China (5 Jan. – 3 Feb.), the 2nd month of China (6 Mar. – 4 Apr.), the 5th month of China (6 Jun. - 6 Jul) and in the 11th month of China (7 Dec 22 - 5 Jan 23), Be wary of the consequences of both small and large issues. People should avoid going to entertainment venues because there may be illnesses attached to them as gifts.

Health

This year, health concerns should be cautious of workplace and travel accidents, as well as the use of various sharp tools. They should also focus more on intestinal diseases, gastritis, and food poisoning. You must maintain good hygiene and pay close attention to your health, especially in the coming months: the 12th month of China (5 Jan. – 3 Feb.), the 2nd month of China (6 Mar. – 4 Apr.), the 5th month of China (6 Jun. – 6 Jul) and the 11th month of China (7 Dec 22 – 5 Jan 23). Socializing with friends, both drinking and using intoxicating drugs, should be done with caution and moderation; do not allow drunken things to happen or accidents to occur, and be aware of sickness while traveling long distances or visiting strange places.

Year of the HORSE (Gold) | (1990)

" The Horse In the sky" is a person born in the year of the HORSE at the age of 33 years (1990)

Overview

The planet orbiting into your destiny this year is the "Dharma Water Star" for this age. This year may feel as difficult as a horse across a mountain road, both at work and in business. smooth, but after passing through this mountain, you will enter a civilized city. As a result, you should be diligent and never give up on your self-improvement. Maintain awareness of the current situation and the ability to change your job or care at any time. You'll have a chance to succeed as long as you don't stick to it. Furthermore, liaison with foreign countries will be beneficial. You should work hard to improve your chances, just as you would if you were laying down floor tiles one by one. It will be simple to walk down this path in the future, so don't be discouraged. You should make time at the start of the year to pay homage to the Tai Tai gods and make merit. Things that aren't going smoothly will come to an end, allowing you to avoid disaster.

Career and Business

The career horoscope for this year is falling, so now is the time to practice. Please keep your commitment if you are looking for a new business to expand. Even if the journey is difficult, you will eventually succeed. The expectation of academic results at home and abroad is within reach. Because you are in the world of work and commerce. I also ask that you take care of the work in your responsibilities. To keep up with world trends, you must constantly add new knowledge to yourself in addition to maintaining constant diligence. It is critical to not look past an adult's head to progress and grow. Those of you who are trading this year must be more diligent, hope a lot, be diligent, and develop yourself with sales to run. But be careful in the months when business and trade will cause problems, such as the 12th month of China (5 Jan. - 3 Feb.), and the 2nd month of China (6 Mar. - 4 Apr.). The 5th month of China (6 Jun. - 6 Jul.) and the 11th month of China (7 Dec. 22 - 5 Jan. 23) on various contract documents. You must read the details carefully.

As for the month in which your work and trade will have a smooth and bright direction, namely the 1st month of China (4 Feb. – 5 Mar.), the 6th month of China (7 Jul. – 7 Aug.), the 8th month of China (8 Sep. – 7 Oct.) and 9th month of China (8 Oct. – 6 Nov.).

Financial

The fortunes and financial fortunes of this year are moderately depressed. As a result, you must carefully plan your income, expenses, and revolving funds. As a result, it will go by quickly and easily. Anything not necessary should be saved, and more income should be generated to cover unexpected expenses. Do not be greedy when gambling; instead, gamble, measure your luck in various matters, and do not force yourself to follow. Avoiding investment-intensive businesses is one of the business ideas that you are not good at or do not have sufficient knowledge and expertise in. Especially during the month when the financial star is down, including the 12th month of China (5 Jan. – 3 Feb.), the 2nd month of China (6 Mar. – 4 Apr.), the 5th month of China (6 Jun. – 6 Jul.) and the 11th month of China (7 Dec. 22 – 5 Jan. 23). You should avoid lending money to others and get any guarantees and be careful not to lose money in unexpected matters.

The month that is destined for the fortune of your destiny's finances Both age cycles flow smoothly, including 1st month of China (4 Feb. – 5 Mar.), 6th month of China (7 Jul. – 7 Aug.), 8th month of China (8 Sep. – 7 Oct.) and the 9th month of China (8 Oct. – 6 Nov.).

Family

These two age cycles were not so smooth within the Lord's family. Although the first six months were peaceful. But there's always been something that makes me uneasy in the last six months. Be aware that unexpected events that may occur to family members as a result of the villain's influence will have an impact on the health and safety of people in the home. However, it is fortunate that in the future, auspicious stars will appear, and the earth will shine, allowing the burden to be lighter. However, you should not be underestimated when entering the following months, which are the 12th month of china (5 Jan. – 3 Feb.), the 2nd month of china (6 Mar. – 4 Apr.), the 5th month of china (6 Jun. – 6 Jul.) and the 11th month of China (7 Dec 22 – 5 Jan 23) are concerned about accidents that may occur within the home and injure family members Both should increase their care and attention to the elderly's health.

Love

The love story of the year is sweet and cheerful. You will be attractive and affectionate to the opposite sex. Those who are single have a high chance of finding a soulmate if they are not tired of love. But please take the time to carefully examine each other's hearts. Because you will interact with the opposite sex more than once. Before agreeing to join the marriage, consider the inherently right person. The month in which love is prone to conflicts and resentment, is the 12th month of China (5 Jan. - 3 Feb.), the 2nd month of China (6 Mar. - 4 Apr), and the 5th month of China. (6 Jun. – 6 Jul.) and the 11th month of China (7 Dec. 22 – 5 Jan. 23) that the Year of the Horse's destiny must be strong around this age. Do not interfere with other people's love. And beware of third parties interfering in the middle to misinterpret, and beware of disagreements that will lead to serious arguments that will escalate into a problem.

Health

For the Year of the Horse, who is affected by the combined powers, one should not underestimate the accident both at work and on the road. Being injured and bruised in the body, or being sick but refusing to go to the doctor. Take care not to let bacteria build up and spread into a more serious disease later on. As a result, you should keep a close eye on your health. Especially during the month in which destiny must add special attention, such as the

12th month of China (5 Jan. – 3 Feb.), the 2nd month of China (6 Mar. – 4 Apr.), the 5th month of China (6 Jun. – 6 Jul.) and the 11th month of China (7 Dec. 22 – 5 Jan. 23). Furthermore, if you consume alcohol or other intoxicants, you should not drive a vehicle. Be wary of mishaps.

Chinese Astrology Horoscope for Each Month

Month 12 in the Tiger Year (6 Jan 23 - 3 Feb 23)
Your horoscope for the Year of the Horse is fluctuating this year, so you should be careful to maintain a level of responsibility in all responsible activities. Thinking, reading, working, or progressing on any subject. Be wary of being harassed or hurt by gossip.

Despite the auspicious stars orbiting to help, this period has returned to face monsoon problems, including trade. However, this assistance will only provide temporary relief. As a result, you must be diligent, determined, and self-sufficient. Here are some things you should do this month: work or look for work It should be done straightforwardly.

Don't be a liar. You will be caught and will not be able to avoid the lawsuit.

The financial horoscope is normal at this time. As for the money from the unsteady fortune, there are gains and losses, plus or minus, and it may not be worth the principal. As a result, it should be cost-effective to fasten the seat belt based on the sufficiency principle.

You should be aware of unforeseen events or accidents that occur to family members if there is no peace in the family. Keep an eye on the health of the elderly in your home, as well as your illnesses. As a result, they must be stricter with themselves and the family's elders.

As for love, there may be some misunderstandings at this stage, so let's coordinate the relationship patiently and calmly.

The relationships with family and friends are strained. For a while, you may need to keep your distance and refrain from interfering in other people's problems.

Traveling and driving in good health; however, be cautious of accidents.

Starting a new job, including investment, is not a good idea, and should be postponed.

Support Days: 4 Jan., 8 Jan., 12 Jan., 16 Jan., 20 Jan., 24 Jan., 28 Jan.
Lucky Days: 1 Jan., 13 Jan., 25 Jan.
Misfortune Days: 6 Jan., 18 Jan., 30 Jan.
Bad Days: 7 Jan., 9 Jan., 19 Jan., 21 Jan., 31 Jan.

Month 1 in the Rabbit Year (4 Feb 23 - 5 Mar 23)
As you begin this month, the first thing you should consider is setting goals for your work activities throughout the year. The most important factor is to plan the budget, as well as the work systems and personnel that must be prepared. This is because this month is yet another month for work and business to have patrons to help along with the auspicious

constellation's influence, which is still a boost. Pushing for the smooth implementation of various activities, seeing the progress.

What you should do during this time is think about your goals and fill in the gaps. And it's critical if your interpersonal skills are lacking. Being polite, smiling, and remaining humble will benefit you.

With the flow of money, the financial star shone brightly. Direct income is still coming in normally. When it comes to luck, fortune floats when there is some sporadic, and if you know how to stop, you will not lose.

Family life is at peace when ties within the home are strengthened, people get to know each other, and people respect each other.

Those who have been in love for a long time will have an auspicious occasion for engagement or marriage during this period. Those who do not have a partner will have the opportunity to meet the right person, and you must move forward in the relationship diligently to have the right to be fulfilled.

There are no concerns about your health during this period.

There is a good return on entering into joint ventures, starting a new job, and investing in various investments this month.

Support Days: 1 Feb., 5 Feb., 9 Feb., 13 Feb., 17 Feb., 21 Feb., 25 Feb.
Lucky Days: 6 Feb., 18 Feb.
Misfortune Days: 11 Feb., 23 Feb.
Bad Days: 2 Feb., 12 Feb., 14 Feb., 24 Feb., 26 Feb.

Month 2 in the Rabbit Year (6 Mar 23 - 5 Apr 23)
This month, your destiny criterion is threatened by monsoon waves. It is also where the evil stars congregate, causing the financial deficit. Obstacles and problems abound at work. Many activities will not go as smoothly as you would like. As a result, in the field of

commerce during this time, you must exercise greater caution. Several factors should be carefully considered before investing.

On this occasion, you should focus on minor details without allowing your blood to rush to your face. Big things are perceived as small. Stuck in work and business, there are problems if necessary, and no solution can be found. needing to seek assistance from relatives It's not necessarily a bad thing.

This salary horoscope indicates that expenditures exceed income and that liquidity does not flow smoothly. As a result, you should avoid gambling and gambling, including lending money to others or taking out guarantees on anyone's behalf. Everything that can be saved should be saved.

There will be disagreements in the family during this time. Be wary of elders or their servants causing problems and causing trouble to avoid losing money.

In this month of love, you must trust, be patient, resist provocations, and refuse to listen to one side.

If you are not feeling well, you should see a doctor right away. To diagnose and treat accidents, and to avoid being careless with them,

In terms of relatives and stock investments, starting a new job, including various investments, should be avoided during this month.

Support Days: 1 Mar, 5 Mar., 9 Mar., 13 Mar., 17 Mar., 21 Mar., 25 Mar., 29 Mar.
Lucky Days: 2 Mar, 14 Mar., 26 Mar.
Misfortune Days: 7 Mar, 19 Mar., 31 Mar.
Bad Days: 8 Mar, 10 Mar., 20 Mar., 22 Mar.

Month 3 in the Rabbit Year (6 Apr 23 - 5 May 23)
Even in this month, the road of life of the Year of the Horse's destiny will have a better direction, obstacles, and pressing problems will find helpers to relieve suffering. However, because the aftermath of the remaining dark energy is that your mind lacks self-esteem, some activities may forget the act of improper behavior, obstructing to lose the opportunity to move forward. As a result, I ask you to set aside the principles of self-destruction and focus your attention on yourself.

This time found a supportive patron in the field of work and business. Increased diligence in producing results and making sales to make up for a lost time.

This month, here's what you should do. Being humble, being mindful at work, and staying out of other people's problems. It will make many activities run more smoothly. not wishing to be envious of

Financial horoscope, even if you have a good income, be careful not to gamble with luck, as this will only result in losses.

During this time, family life is peaceful. There will be long-distance visitors or good news from afar, but valuables should be kept safe in the house. When you leave the house, be cautious of pickpockets or having to pay because the items in the house are damaged and must be replaced.

When the love tree bears its fruit, life is easier for those who are still single. Those of you who are in love are assisted by an adult to smooth out the expectations.

During this period of health, be cautious of infectious diseases and allergies, and avoid foods like grilling, grilling, and barbeque, which will accumulate and cause disease, which will be a major problem later.

Investing in stocks this month can bring you good fortune and luck.

Support Days: 2 Apr., 6 Apr., 10 Apr., 14 Apr., 18 Apr., 22 Apr., 26 Apr., 30 Apr.
Lucky Days: 7 Apr., 19 Apr.
Misfortune Days: 12 Apr., 24Apr.
Bad Days: 1 Apr., 3 Apr., 13 Apr., 15 Apr., 25 Apr., 27 Apr.

Month 4 in the Rabbit Year (6 May 23 - 5 Jun 23)
Your destiny, born in the Year of the Horse, enters this month, and finds the Sompong line, even to reduce problems and obstacles at work to appear lighter. However, the unfortunate power of the evil star moving to radiate radius remains, particularly the influence of the demon stars "Pae Hou" (White Tiger) and "Peak Auk" (Crossing the sky). As a result, fate should be cautious of accidents while traveling and the dangers of using road vehicles.

The direction of trade work during this period was somewhat erratic due to the situation and surrounding factors. However, in the dark, you will find helpers, so this is a good opportunity to find bugs and fix them quickly to expand trade. Increase sales or build a portfolio. Convert a crisis into a chance to advance your career.

On this occasion, you should carefully plan your finances and review the placement of the right people for the job.

This salary fortune's fortune, income, and expenses are all equal. However, there are ways to earn a lot of money by increasing your income; however, you should also keep it for emergencies.

On the family front, the incident restored peace and harmony.

There will be times when you misunderstand each other in love. As a result, be mindful, avoid being stubborn, and separate work and personal time.

Good family and friends will meet friends to support share investment, starting a new job, and other investments. There is a small chance of getting hurt this month.

Support Days: 4 May., 8 May., 12 May., 16 May., 20 May., 24 May., and 28 May.
Lucky Days: 1 May., 13 May., and 25 May.
Misfortune Days: 6 May., 18 May., 30 May.
Bad Days: 7 May., 9 May., 19 May., 21 May., 31 May.

Month 5 in the Rabbit Year (6 Jun 23 - 6 Jul 23)

This month, the road of life met the force of destiny, and it fell. Workplace challenges and conflicts will begin to emerge. You may sustain injury if you are not cautious.

This month's job and trade prospects are bleak; there will be numerous errors. Doing various activities, don't be impatient, do whatever you want, and you'll find damage.

What you should be aware of on this occasion is that in all activities, do not be selfish or considerate of acquaintances. But must take into account cause and effect It will significantly reduce the likelihood of being taken advantage of.

Horoscopes, this salary has been lost; be wary of working capital, a lack of liquidity, and new investments. You should wait before becoming aware of accounting and tax calculation errors or problems with government agencies.

Please calm down in the family during this period of peace, as this may cause arguments with the people in the family. Be wary of a lawsuit from a minor who is the cause, as well as unexpected events.

Disagreements are easy to argue about in the love horoscope. Please give careful consideration to other people's hearts. Things will work out if you know how to forgive. Visitors to entertainment venues during this time should exercise caution to avoid contracting the disease and should avoid becoming involved in other people's families.

During this period of health, there is a criterion to fall asleep, be careful of overdoing, hard work, and obsessing over some problems, it will accumulate stress. Often have headaches and insomnia, beware of accidents during work and travel.

The investment in stocks this month is still not bright. We have to wait.

Support Days: 1 Jun., 5 Jun., 9 Jun., 13 Jun., 17 Jun., 21 Jun., 25 Jun., 29 Jun.
Lucky Days: 6 Jun., 18 Jun., 30 Jun
Misfortune Days: 11 Jun., 23 Jun.
Bad Days: 2 Jun., 12 Jun., 14 Jun., 24 Jun., 26 Jun.

Month 6 in the Rabbit Year (7 Jul 23 - 7 Aug 23)
This month is auspicious because many auspicious stars are moving into orbit to shine above the zodiac house. Many problems that have accumulated over the previous month will be reduced, obstacles and trade problems will

be resolved, and work will be found in this phase to be smooth and successful.

On this occasion, you should evaluate the previous year's performance. Outline the successful path or paths to plan a strategy for moving forward. However, if something goes wrong, identify the root cause and use it as a learning experience to avoid making the same mistakes again.

This period of good fortune is likely to leak and lose quickly. You should still keep a close eye on your spending. Take good care of money and gold for those who wish to be wealthy. Enough to put a smile on my face and money in my pocket. However, being greedy will result in a loss.

During this time, the family is still happy and smooth.

The body's health still requires constant maintenance. It doesn't matter if you have to sleep for a long time if you act on your heart.

The relationship for the destiny who is still single is progressing. This month is easy and enjoyable for those who have loved ones and spouses.

Relatives and friends are in good health and have the opportunity to travel together to strengthen bonds. They will also have the opportunity to co-host a merit-making event.

Starting a new job after investing in stocks including various investments this month is possible, and will result in a good income.

Support Days: 3 Jul., 7 Jul., 11 Jul., 15 Jul., 19 Jul., 23 Jul., 27 Jul., 31 Jul.
Lucky Days: 12 Jul., 24 Jul.
Misfortune Days: 5 Jul., 17 Jul., 29 Jul.
Bad Days: 6 Jul., 8 Jul., 18 Jul., 20 Jul., 30 Jul.

Month 7 in the Rabbit Year (8 Aug 23 - 7 Sep 23)
This month's destiny criteria are good and evil. You should be aware that working capital will be insufficiently liquid. It appears that

expenses and damages are unforeseeable, and patients should be wary of diseases that will beset them. But in terms of work, including business, everything is fine. This is another month in which you should take advantage of the opportunity to improve your sales results and move closer to becoming a market leader.

What you should do on this occasion is spend. should adhere to saving measures and closely monitor working capital liquidity Do not be overly greedy with someone else's fortune. If you are greedy, your fortune will vanish. You should take precautions to stay healthy and fit.

Even though income is coming in from a variety of sources, this salary is horoscope. However, there will be a cause of property loss in an unrelated matter or compensation for damages. And, during this time, you should avoid letting others borrow money or sign documents certifying guarantees on your behalf, and you should avoid gambling with any luck.

There was still a commotion in the family's home. Be careful not to argue with words that were not well thought out. As a result, it should be treasured and cared for. This month, we must continue to be cautious of accidents. Be wary of minors or dependents who cause havoc.

On the romantic front, the relationship has improved during this time. However, you must maintain conscious control over your body and mind.

The outlook for stock investments is bleak.

Support Days: 4 Aug., 8 Aug., 12 Aug., 16 Aug., 20 Aug., 24 Aug., 28 Aug.
Lucky Days: 5 Aug., 17 Aug., 29 Aug.
Misfortune Days: 10 Aug., 22 Aug.
Bad Days: 1 Aug., 11 Aug., 13 Aug., 23 Aug., 25 Aug

Month 8 in the Rabbit Year (8 Sep 23 - 7 Oct 23)
Conflicts arose in the lives of those born in the Year of the Horse this month. As a result, you should exercise caution at work, as disagreements are common. Arguing occurs frequently, causing work to stall and progress to be hampered.

This period has not been easy in terms of work, including business. Conflicts with colleagues must be avoided by destiny. Patience and compromise are sometimes required to bring an incident to a close. It is preferable to use emotions to allow things to happen and to bind the accumulated pain as a grudge for future hurting each other.

On this occasion, you should be patient, try to suppress your emotions, and be open to other people's perspectives. Do not be aggressive; spitting poisonous speech at others will result in endless arguments.

This salary horoscope is typical. You still have a steady income, but your expenses are rising.

The money from fortune may pass through a small number of hands. As a result, you should not gamble, speculate, or measure your luck in various fields.

There is strife in the family. Be wary of disagreements escalating into a major issues.

The opposite sex will take care of the good in love. It's almost time for the hard work of the love tree to bear fruit.

During this time, be cautious of gastritis, intestinal disease, high blood pressure, and cerebrovascular disease. You should see a doctor about getting blood tests. Seek immediate medical attention if any abnormalities appear.

When traveling, both near and far, you must be cautious of accidents.

Investments in stocks, including various investments this month, should be avoided before being safe for relatives.

Support Days: 1 Sep, 5 Sep., 9 Sep, 13 Sep, 17 Sep., 21 Sep., 25 Sep., 29 Sep
Lucky Days: 10 Sep, 22 Sep.
Misfortune Days: 3 Sep, 15 Sep., 27 Sep.
Bad Days: 4 Sep, 6 Sep., 16 Sep., 18 Sep, 28 Sep., 30 Sep

Month 9 in the Rabbit Year (8 Oct 23 - 6 Nov 23)
This month, your destiny born in the Year of the Horse has reached the alliance line, resulting in powerful support that has soared back up. It also received a ray of light from many auspicious stars that passed through the house of fate. As a result, you will be able to find patrons easily this month, both at work and at home. As a result, the issue of work and business is a golden opportunity that you must seize to expand trade. It should be accelerated to create work or to increase sales.

This month, you should focus on work and sales because adults, whether bosses or coworkers have each other's hearts and minds; there is no jealousy. It is a good opportunity to move forward with outstanding projects if only to assist and support.

This salary horoscope has a high level of liquidity. Direct cash inflows continue to be substantial. However, the money from the fortune Should be careful not to become too big. You should only spend in moderation. Otherwise, you will have problems and suffer later.

There may be an auspicious event in the house, as well as the opportunity to add new members or relocate to a new place of employment.

horoscope for a sweet love loving spouse and the opportunity to travel or participate in activities together

In good health, but avoid drinking alcohol because driving will be dangerous.

This rhythm's horoscope indicates a favorable month. You can collaborate on projects or invest in stocks together.

The start of a new job, along with various investments, will yield a good return.

Support Days: 3 Oct., 7 Oct., 11 Oct., 15 Oct., 19 Oct., 23 Oct., 27 Oct., 31 Oct.
Lucky Days: 4 Oct., 16 Oct., 27 Oct.
Misfortune Days: 9 Oct., 21 Oct.
Bad Days: 10 Oct., 12 Oct., 22 Oct., 24 Oct.

Month 10 in the Rabbit Year (7 Nov 23 - 6 Dec 23)
This month, your destiny has shifted to the front lines of business and business will find competitors. It will put additional pressure on you to work harder. They gain market share by cutting prices, stealing customers, and employing various strategies. On this occasion, you should be more attentive and cautious in your work. To avoid mistakes in both products and people You should also have a solid financial plan. To reserve for liquidity, it should

postpone expenditures that can extend the payment period in advance. It is critical not to continue visiting customers or strengthening relationships with regular contacts.

This stagnant salary will have an impact on liquidity, which will also stagnate, causing a slew of issues. As a result, you should follow the sufficiency principle. Every activity should be strict on saving and finding ways to prevent money leakage, as well as closely managing income and expenses. You should also not allow anyone to borrow money or accept guarantees on your behalf. You should not try your luck or engage in the illegal trade investment business.

This is a peaceful and smooth time in the family.

In terms of love, you will be drawn to the attention of the opposite sex. For singles who are waiting for the right time. This month is a good time to ask for love from the other person.

Even if you get sick, you will be able to find a good doctor and medicine to help you heal.

Relatives and friends are helpful, but investment stocks can help you start a new job. This month, you should be wary of losses and allow yourself to be duped.

Support Days: 4 Nov., 8 Nov., 12 Nov., 16 Nov., 20 Nov., 24 Nov., 28 Nov.

Lucky Days: 9 Nov., 21 Nov.
Misfortune Days: 2 Nov., 14 Nov., 26 Nov.
Bad Days: 3 Nov., 5 Nov., 15 Nov., 17 Nov., 27 Nov., 29 Nov.

Month 11 in the Rabbit Year (7 Dec 23 - 5 Jan 24)
The destiny criterion for this month has shifted to the Chong resistance level. Furthermore, numerous evil stars are destroying them. Problems of various sizes rage with each step they take. Unevenness is a common problem.

This month, you should pay special attention to personnel management at work, including commercial matters. Arrange for the right people to do the job to increase efficiency and have a lot more work. They should also be familiar with market trends and your target customers. Do not release or release the product at an inconvenient time and does not meet the needs of consumers, it risks losing and being hurt.

This salary horoscope is moderate; money from fortune is sufficient; however, be cautious; there is a limit to losing more. It is preferable to avoid gambling luck. This month should not be taken for granted, and you should not be greedy.

In this period of health, be cautious of injury from driving or using a car on the road, and always practice hygienic living and eating.

There is still chaos in the family; be wary of lost or stolen valuables and elders who cause trouble.

On the romantic front, you and your spouse frequently disagree. During this month, you should pay closer attention to avoid misunderstandings that lead to arguments.

Investing in stocks, starting a new job, and making various investments this month are all examples of selfishness.

Support Days: 2 Dec., 6 Dec., 10 Dec., 14 Dec., 18 Dec., 22 Dec., 26 Dec, 30 Dec.
Lucky Days: 3 Dec., 15 Dec., 27 Dec.
Misfortune Days: 8 Dec., 20 Dec.
Bad Days: 9 Dec., 11 Dec., 21 Dec., 23 Dec.

Amulet for The Year of the Horse
"Dizhang Aung on a lion"

Those born in the year of the Horse this year should establish and worship sacred objects "Dizhang Aung on a lion" to enhance your fortune by placing it on your desk or cash desk to ask His Majesty for mercy to protect your destiny from all dangers, eliminating unfortunate things, and bringing wealth and peace to you and your family members.

(Take note of the direction in which the sacred object should be placed.) It is visible at the end of your life cycle.)

Chapter one of the Department of Advanced Feng Shui discusses the gods who will come down to reside in the annual Mi Keng (Destiny House), who are the gods who can bring both good and bad to the year's destiny. When this occurs, the worship is supplemented by gods who come down to reside regularly in the year of your birth. As a result, it is thought to produce the best results and has the greatest impact on you. To rely on the gods' prestige, he assists in protecting while his destiny is low and misfortune is reduced. At the same time, I'd like to wish you blessings to help inspire the smooth running of your business as you seek to bring prosperity and prosperity to yourself and your family.

Those born in the Year of the Pig or Mi Keng (House of Destiny) fall under the Foolish zodiac sign. This year is filled with chaos and problems that you must solve without fail. Furthermore, his birth year falls on the "Heng" digit, indicating that it is the year of the union. As a result, he meets the criteria for being oppressed by close friends by being taken by people to steal his fortune. They must be cautious not to be corrupted by their own decisions. If you expect great results in the second half of the year, keep trying to go as planned. Traveling to other countries will yield positive results. The lobbying move away from the old location will be beneficial, but the finances have not been flowing smoothly. There are still things in the family that give him a headache. You should avoid interfering too much with others this year. Be cautious of being bullied. In good health, but be cautious of accidents while participating in sports or exercising. If you believe that setting up amulets and wearing amulets will help you overcome your misfortune, you should do so. "Dizhang Aung on a lion" to seek His Majesty's help in breaking the bad luck. Practicing career advancement, wishing for anything, wishing to achieve the desired results.

"Phra Tee Chang Phosak" or "Dizhang Aung Bodhisattva on a lion" is a great Bodhisattva who has mercy and supreme prestige with a determination to save all beings from suffering in all worlds, both heaven, and Hell. He is a Bodhisattva who is highly revered in China, Japan, Thailand, and Cambodia because he is a graceful monk who holds Anyone who worships Him will find good people and a good environment. Have the chance to meet new friends and guide them to happiness and noble wealth. Parents who pray and worship Him will raise their children in obedience. It is simple to raise, obey the teachings, and avoid dangers.

Those born in the year of the horse should also wear a sacred pendant. "Dizhang Aung on a lion" was worn around his neck or carried with him when he traveled outside the house, near and far, to enrich his destiny with auspicious treasures. To be effective, there must be prosperity and progress in business, business, business, family peace and happiness throughout the year, and greater productivity and speed than ever before.

Good Direction: Northeast, Northwest, and South
Bad Direction: North
Lucky Colors: Red, Pink, Orange, and Green.
Lucky Times: 1100 – 11.59, 13.00 – 14.59, 19.00 – 20.59.
Bad Times: 05.00 – 06.59, 09.00 – 10.59., 23.00 – 00.59

Good Luck For 2023